Project Weather

THE PROJECT MAKERS

Philip Steele

WINDMILL
BOOKS

Published in 2020 by Windmill Books,
an imprint of Rosen Publishing
29 East 21st Street, New York, NY 10010

Copyright © 2020 Miles Kelly Publishing

Publishing Director: Belinda Gallagher
Creative Director: Jo Cowan
Editorial Director: Rosie Neave
Design Manager: Joe Jones
Consultant: Anne Rooney
Indexer: Marie Lorimer
Image Manager: Liberty Newton
Production: Elizabeth Collins, Jennifer Brunwin-Jones
Reprographics: Stephan Davis
Assets: Lorraine King
Cataloging-in-Publication Data

Names: Steele, Philip.
Title: Project weather / Philip Steele.
Description: New York : Windmill Books, 2020. | Series: The project makers
| Includes index.
Identifiers: ISBN 9781538392409 (pbk.) | ISBN 9781725393080 (library bound)
| ISBN 9781538392416 (6 pack)
Subjects: LCSH: Weather--Experiments--Juvenile literature. | Meteorology--Experim
-Juvenile literature. | Weather--Juvenile literature. | Science projects--Juvenile litera
Classification: LCC QC981.3 S744 2019 | DDC 551.5078--dc23

Manufactured in the United States of America

CPSIA Compliance Information: Batch #BW20WM:
For Further Information contact Rosen Publishing,
New York, New York at 1-800-237-9932

How to use the projects

This book is packed full of amazing facts about weather. There are also 11 cool projects, designed to make the subject come alive.

Before you start a project:

- Always ask an adult to help you.

- Read the instructions carefully.

- Gather all the supplies you need.

- Clear a surface to work on and cover it with newspaper.

- Wear an apron or old T-shirt to protect your clothing.

Notes for helpers:

- Children will need supervision for the projects, usually because they require the use of scissors, or preparation beforehand.

- Read the instructions together before starting and help to gather the equipment.

IMPORTANT NOTICE
The publisher and author cannot be held responsible for any injuries, damage, or loss resulting from the use or misuse of any of the information in this book.

SAFETY FIRST!
Be careful when using glue or anything sharp, such as scissors.

How to use:
If your project doesn't work the first time, try again – just have fun!

Cloud in a jar

Supplies:
The equipment should be easy to find, around the house or from a craft store. Always ask before using materials from home.

Numbered stages:
Each stage of the project is numbered and the illustrations will help you. Follow the stages in the order shown to complete the project. If glue or paint is used, make sure it is dry before moving on to the next stage.

Try making your own cloud.

SUPPLIES

glass jar with metal lid • just-boiled water
• ice cubes • timer • aerosol hairspray

HOW TO MAKE

1. Pour the water into the jar, to a depth of about 1 inch (2 cm). Swish the water around the jar to warm the sides of the jar.

2. Turn the jar's lid upside down, place the ice cubes in it, and put it on top of the jar.

3. After 20 seconds, take the lid away and squirt a small amount of hairspray into the jar.

4. Replace the lid with the ice still in it. Tiny water drops condense and form a "cloud".

5. When the cloud has formed, take off the lid and let it escape.

HOW IT WORKS

As the warm water evaporates, the gas rises and is cooled by the ice. It condenses around the aerosol particles, just as it would around specks of dust in nature.

CONTENTS

What is weather?

Our planet is surrounded by air. This layer of gases is known as the atmosphere, and the way it behaves from one day to the next is called the weather. Will it be rainy, sunny, windy — or will it snow? The weather changes all the time as heat from the Sun interacts with land, sea, and air.

Feel the warmth

Earth spins as it travels around the Sun. By **day** the side facing the Sun is warm and light. By **night** the side facing away is cool and dark.

Earth's tilted angle means that in many parts of the world we have **seasons**.

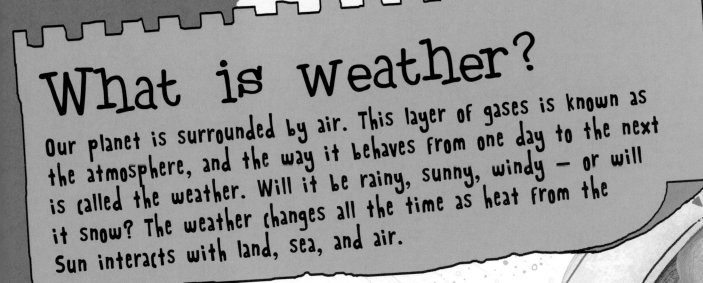

Northern Spring

Northern Summer

Northern Autumn

Northern Winter

The part tilted towards the Sun has warm **summer** days. The part tilted away has cold **winter** days.

What is climate?

Weather patterns over a long period are known as the climate. Weather scientists, called meteorologists, record the weather in a place each day for many years so that they can see changes in the climate.

Weather balloons carry instruments that collect data like wind speed and send it back to meteorologists on the ground.

The world's weather

Earth's polar regions get little direct sunshine, so they stay cold. The lands around the equator, in the middle of the planet, get the full blast of the Sun's rays and stay hot. This temperature difference affects winds and ocean currents, creating global weather patterns.

MID-LATITUDE

POLAR

As the atmosphere circulates around our spinning planet, it creates regular wind patterns. These form "belts" around Earth, two of which meet at the ITCZ (see above).

4

The higher you go above Earth's surface, the colder it gets. Air pressure drops, too. Scientists call the lowest level of the atmosphere the troposphere (1), and it contains most of the air and water vapor that keeps us alive. The levels above it are called the stratosphere (2), the mesosphere (3), and the thermosphere (4).

POLAR

MID-LATITUDE

INTERTROPICAL
CONVERGENCE
ZONE (ITCZ)

The light show known as the Aurora Borealis (or Northern Lights) is caused by charged particles from the Sun colliding with gases high in Earth's atmosphere. This photo was taken from the International Space Station.

Chart the Weather

Ask an adult for help!

Make and display a picture chart to show the daily weather conditions.

SUPPLIES

large paper plate • ruler • felt-tip pens
• small sheet of card stock • scissors
• metal paper fastener • notebook

HOW TO MAKE

1. Use a black felt-tip pen and ruler to divide the paper plate into six equal portions.

2. Draw a weather symbol on each portion and color it in. The symbols should represent types of weather your area gets. For example cloudy, sunny, rainy, windy, snowy, stormy.

3. Draw and cut out an arrow from the card stock. Fix it to the picture side of the plate with the paper fastener and make sure it can turn.

HOW TO USE

Display the chart on the wall. Notice what the weather is like each day. At the end of the day, turn the arrow so your chart matches the day's weather.

Write the date and the symbol you recorded in the notebook. At the end of one month, count how many times you used each symbol. Can you see any patterns?

Blow by blow

Earth's atmosphere isn't the same all over. Some air masses are warm, others are cold. Some are at high pressure, others are at low pressure — meaning they press against surfaces with varying force. Winds are caused by differences in temperature and pressure that make air rush from one area into another.

Where the wind blows

Earth's spin shifts the direction of wind patterns around the globe. Winds passing over the surface of the planet are affected by the land and water beneath them. Hot, dry air that travels over a cold sea will soon cool down and pick up evaporating water.

The huge whirling disc of thunderclouds that makes up a hurricane is hundreds of miles in diameter. The huge scale of this weather system only becomes clear when seen from space.

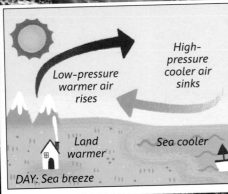

Low-pressure warmer air rises
High-pressure cooler air sinks
Land warmer
Sea cooler
DAY: Sea breeze

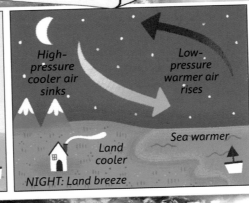

High-pressure cooler air sinks
Low-pressure warmer air rises
Land cooler
Sea warmer
NIGHT: Land breeze

At the coast, the difference in temperature between air over land and air over the sea creates sea breezes (as cool air moves from sea to land) during the day. The opposite happens at night.

Up and down

As well as passing over the surface of the planet, air also moves upward and downward. Warm air rises, but as it gets higher it cools and begins to sink back to the surface. These movements of air bring in low pressure, with a risk of rain. Different kinds of air masses bring different kinds of weather.

A cold front is the border between an advancing mass of cold air and the mass of warm air it is replacing.

Warm air

Advancing cold air

Build a weather vane

Make a weather vane to show the direction of the wind.

Ask an adult for help!

HOW TO USE
Take your weather vane outside when the wind is blowing. Use your compass to align the base. Which direction does the arrow point to?

SUPPLIES

thick card stock • felt-tip pen • big plastic plate • big yogurt cup with lid • ruler • modeling clay • small pebbles • glue • pencil with eraser • thin card stock • scissors • pin • straw • magnetic compass

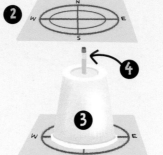

Westerly winds come from the west, easterlies from the east, and so on.

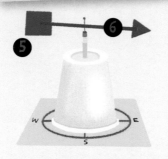

WHAT TO DO

1. Use the pen to draw a big circle in the middle of the card stock, using the plate as a guide. Then use the lid of the yogurt cup as a guide to draw a small circle within the big circle.

2. Use the ruler to divide the circles into quarters. Label them NORTH, SOUTH, EAST, and WEST.

3. Fill the base of the cup with modeling clay. Fill the rest with pebbles. Fit the lid back on and glue the cup upside down to the card stock.

4. Push the pencil through the center of the pot, so its point sticks in the modeling clay.

5. Cut a triangle and a square from the thin card stock, and insert into small cuts made into each end of the straw.

6. Pin the straw to the pencil eraser, making sure it can spin freely.

Wild and whirling

Hurricanes and other violent tropical storms form above the world's warm oceans. They pick up vast amounts of water vapor, which falls as heavy rain. They whirl around a central calm spot, known as the eye.

Northern tropical storms blow counterclockwise, while southern ones blow clockwise. The direction is caused by Earth's spin.

Too cool!

The fastest winds of all are called **jet streams.** They move high in the atmosphere, 5.6–10 miles (9–16 km) above Earth's surface.

Jet streams travel at up to **200 miles** (320 km) per hour, the same speed as a race car!

During the winter, jet streams are nearer the equator, and they travel **faster** than during the **summer.**

Water goes around

Earth can support life because it has huge amounts of water. It has salty oceans and seas, and freshwater lakes and rivers. Water moves endlessly from land and sea into the air and back again. This process is called the water cycle. It helps create our weather systems.

Cloud

Sun

Precipitation

Wonder water

Water covers about **70 percent** of **Earth's** surface.

The temperature at which water boils changes depending on how high you are — it boils at **212°F (100°C)** at sea level, but just **154.4°F (68°C)** on the top of **Mount Everest!**

Water is one of only a few substances that **expands** as it **freezes.** That's why pipes can burst during cold weather.

Water vapor is carried upward by warm currents of air. As the gas rises, it cools and condenses, turning back into tiny drops of liquid and forming clouds.

Evaporation

What is water?

Water is a colorless liquid made of two elements – hydrogen and oxygen. Its scientific formula is H_2O. It exists in three forms. It can be a liquid, called simply water. It can freeze into a solid, called ice. It can also turn into an invisible gas, called water vapor.

H O H

Ocean

Water in oceans and lakes evaporates, turning into a gas called water vapor.

River

Freshwater and salt water are home to all sorts of plants and animals.

Vapor

When something that is wet dries out, the water doesn't just disappear. The warmth of the Sun turns the liquid water into a gas. This process is called evaporation.

8

These droplets join together to form bigger drops, which fall to the ground as rain or snow. Scientists call this process precipitation.

Water cycle in action

Try this experiment which shows how the water cycle works.

Ask an adult for help!

SUPPLIES

heatproof cup • heatproof glass • bowl • hot water • plastic wrap • ice cube

WHAT TO DO

1. Place the cup in the bowl. Pour hot water into the bowl, around the base of the cup.

2. Cover the top of the bowl tightly with plastic wrap.

3. Place the ice cube on the plastic wrap just above the cup.

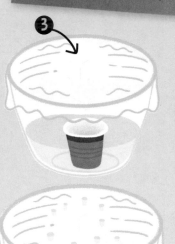

Streams

HOW IT WORKS

The hot water gives off steam. Water vapor gathers on the underside of the plastic wrap. Below the ice, the plastic wrap becomes cold. The water vapor condenses into water drops, which precipitate into the cup.

WHAT CAN WE LEARN?

The hot water is like the ocean when it is warmed by the Sun. As it evaporates, the warm vapor rises. The ice is like high, cool air – it causes the vapor to condense and precipitate.

Most of the rain forms springs, streams, and rivers that flow to the sea.

Lake

Water soaks into the ground, and forms underground pools. If the rock above collapses, the pools are revealed. They are called sinkholes or cenotes.

Ground water

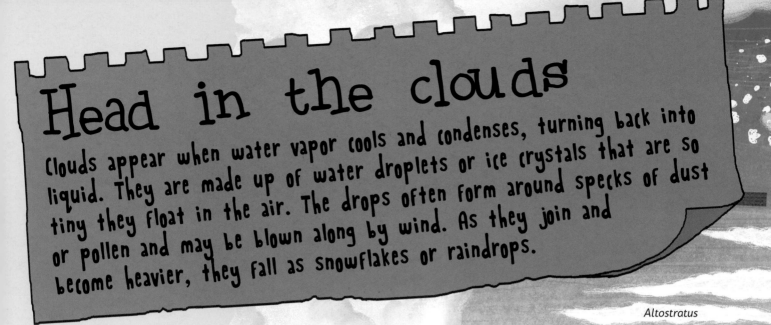

Head in the clouds

Clouds appear when water vapor cools and condenses, turning back into liquid. They are made up of water droplets or ice crystals that are so tiny they float in the air. The drops often form around specks of dust or pollen and may be blown along by wind. As they join and become heavier, they fall as snowflakes or raindrops.

Altostratus

Cumulus

How do clouds form?

Each cloud is a huge mass of tiny drops of liquid water or solid ice crystals.

The tallest clouds, called cumulonimbus, can be 7.5 miles (12 km) high or more!

Cumulonimbus

Clouds are given special scientific names to describe their height and shape.

SHAPEs and sizes

Clouds make all sorts of shapes in the sky, depending on how high they are and on the weather conditions. Some are fluffy and round, while others are spread out, forming layers across the sky.

5. Many droplets combine to form a cloud.

4. The vapor starts to condense around the dust, forming a cloud droplet.

3. Water vapor in the air starts to cool, and sticks to tiny bits of dust in the air.

2. The rising air starts to cool.

1. The Sun warms the ground. Warmed air at ground level starts to rise.

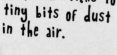
Warm ground

HIGH CLOUDS

Cirrostratus

Cirrocumulus

MIDDLE CLOUDS

Altocumulus

LOW CLOUDS

Stratocumulus

Stratus

Is it a UFO?

No! It's not an alien spacecraft, but a lenticular or disc-shaped cloud. This unusual formation is sometimes seen near mountain ranges.

Lenticular clouds hang in the air without moving.

Cloud in a jar

Ask an adult for help!

Try making your own cloud.

SUPPLIES

glass jar with metal lid • just-boiled water • ice cubes • timer • aerosol hairspray

HOW TO MAKE

1. Pour the water into the jar, to a depth of about 1 inch (2 cm). Swish the water around the jar to warm the sides of the jar.

2. Turn the jar's lid upside down, place the ice cubes in it, and put it on top of the jar.

3. After 20 seconds, take the lid away and squirt a small amount of hairspray into the jar.

4. Replace the lid with the ice still in it. Tiny water drops condense and form a cloud.

5. When the cloud has formed, take off the lid and let it escape.

HOW IT WORKS

As the warm water evaporates, the gas rises and is cooled by the ice. It condenses around the aerosol particles, just as it would around specks of dust in nature.

Rainy days

We may not like rainy days very much, unless they come at the end of a hot, dry spell. But freshwater keeps us all alive. Rainwater makes crops grow, and keeps large areas of our planet fresh and green. It fills rivers and lakes.

How much rain?

A quick shower, a drizzle that lasts all day, or a real downpour? The amount of rain that falls in one place over a period of time is called the rainfall. Some parts of the world have very heavy rainfall, but in other places there is hardly any.

A chimpanzee sits in the pouring rain in Kibale National Park, Uganda, which has two rainy seasons each year.

Rickshaw drivers have to wade through floods on the streets of Dhaka, in Bangladesh.

A wet season

Some rains come each year with the changing seasons. In India, winds coming from the southwest are called monsoons. They blow across the Indian Ocean. Between June and September, they bring torrents of rain to the hot, dry lands of India.

Rain gauge

Rainfall can be collected and measured in a container called a rain gauge.

SUPPLIES

2-liter plastic bottle • scissors • tape • paper ruler • felt-tip pen • trowel

HOW TO MAKE:

1. Cut the bottle in two, about two thirds of the way from the bottom.

2. Turn the top section of the bottle upside down, to make a funnel, slide it inside the bottom section, and tape the two together.

3. Cut out a strip of paper and use the ruler and felt-tip pen to mark out a measurement scale. Stick it to the side of the bottle, with 0 at the bottom. Stick tape over the top of it to keep it dry.

4. Dig a hole on some open ground away from trees and buildings. Place your rain gauge in the hole, with a level base and the top sticking up about 2 inches (5 cm).

Ask an adult for help!

HOW TO USE

Remove your rain gauge from the ground at the same time each day and record the amount of rain collected. Tip the water out and put the gauge back in the ground. If you do this for four weeks, you can add up your measurements to work out the total rainfall for a month.

When you look at a rainbow, you see one color from each raindrop. Drops higher up (1) contribute red light. Drops lower down contribute blue light (2). Drops in between these two heights contribute the other colors.

Too cool!

The wettest place on Earth is Mawsynram in India, which has an average rainfall each year of **467 inches** (11,860 mm). That's as high as...

6 adult people standing on each other's shoulders...

or 4 elephants balancing on top of each other!

13

AROUND THE WORLD

The world can be divided into climate zones, according to regular weather patterns within regions. Each zone supports different plants and animals. The way people live, farm, and dress may also vary greatly from zone to zone.

ARCTIC OCEAN

NORTH AMERICA

ATLANTIC OCEAN

EUROPE

PACIFIC OCEAN

SOUTH AMERICA

SNOW

High altitude lands may have freezing winters. Mountaintops may stay snowy all year round. Plants must be tough to survive.

MEDITERRANEAN

These lands have mild and moist winters but dry, warm, or hot summers.

TROPICAL

On either side of the equator, the lands may be very hot and humid, with high rainfall and lush vegetation.

Weather and the environment

Over the ages, weather conditions have shaped the world we live in. Wind and water wear down or erode the coasts and mountains. Flowing rivers or icy glaciers can create valleys, gorges, or plains. Heavy rainfall creates lush forests, while a lighter rainfall supports grasslands. A lack of rainfall creates hot or cold deserts.

Life on planet Earth has adapted to a wide variety of climate zones.

POLAR

The lands around the poles have very cold, long winters and brief summers. Big areas of ocean freeze over for most of the year.

There are sometimes variations in the usual climate patterns. They can happen quite naturally every few years. One of these is called El Niño. This is a warming of waters in parts of the Pacific Ocean. This upsets the climate around the world, causing floods in some areas and droughts in others.

Ready for the weather

The **polar bear** is well equipped for a polar climate zone.

1 White coat blends in against snow and ice.

2 Thick layers of fat and fur keep out the cold.

3 Large furry feet keep a grip on slippery ice.

The **Arabian camel** is perfectly suited to a desert climate zone.

1 Long eyelashes keep out the sand.

2 Padded feet can walk over hot sand, sharp stones, or thorns.

3 Fatty hump keeps it going when food and water are scarce.

TEMPERATE

ASIA

These lands may include woodland and grassland. A moderate climate and four seasons mean they are suitable for farming.

INDIAN OCEAN

AFRICA

ARID

OCEANIA

Dry lands have little rainfall and may experience extreme cold or heat. Deserts can be windy expanses of sand, ice, gravel, or rock.

RED ALERT!

Bad and fine weather are part of normal conditions on our planet. More unusual weather events are caused by powerful disturbances in Earth's atmosphere. Some types of bad weather are more common in some climate zones than in others. When weather becomes extreme it can be dangerous, putting lives at risk.

WHITE OUT

Blizzards are extreme snowstorms that occur when high winds combine with snow. Gales can whip up snow from the ground or drive snowflakes forward as they fall, creating huge drifts.

An avalanche can hurtle down a mountain at up to 185 miles (300 km) per hour, burying everything under perhaps as much as 11 million tons (10 million t) of snow.

SNOWSLIDE

Avalanches occur when huge banks of snow on mountain slopes become unstable. They may just topple over, or be loosened because of high winds or rising temperatures during a thaw. A mass of tumbling snow and ice can even sweep up trees and rocks as it slides.

A snowplow tries to keep roads open, battling through heavy snow drifts.

DANGER!

The weight of **snow** may cause roofs to collapse and bring down power lines.

Transport comes to a **halt** on slippery, snowy roads.

People **lost** or **trapped** in the snow may suffer from hypothermia (low body temperature) or frostbite (damage to uncovered parts of the body).

A hurricane can leave a trail of destruction up to 300 miles (480 km) across.

STORM SPIRALS

Tropical storms are whirling wheels of rain, wind, and cloud that form over warm seas, smash into coasts, then lose their force. Around the eye, winds rage at up to 155 miles (250 km) per hour. In the Atlantic Ocean they are called hurricanes, in Australia and the Indian Ocean they are called cyclones, and in China and the Pacific they are called typhoons.

TWISTER

The whirling winds known as tornadoes or twisters build up inside storm clouds. They can spin at up to 310 miles (500 km) per hour as they move forward. They form a funnel about 330 feet (100 m) wide, which rips across the landscape. As air pressure drops inside the funnel, the twister sucks up dust and soil.

A single **tornado** in Bangladesh in 1989 destroyed 20 villages, with massive loss of life.

A large area of the US Southwest and Midwest has about 200 twisters a year. No wonder its nickname is Tornado Alley!

Whirling winds can **destroy** buildings, trees and vehicles and cause **loss of life.**

Hurricane-force winds can cause **Shipwrecks** at sea and in harbors.

Once hurricanes hit land they may cause coastal **flooding** and **mudslides.**

WATER WORLD

A heavy rainstorm or a long period of rainy weather can cause floods. Rivers burst their banks and the ground may become so full of water that it cannot soak up any more. A long dry spell can also cause flash floods, because when rain does arrive, the ground is too hard to soak it up. Coastal gales and high tides may drive seawater inland, washing away homes.

A helicopter on a lifesaving mission after Hurricane Katrina left the city of New Orleans underwater in 2005.

When **floodwaters** go down, riverbanks may be covered in a rich, silty mud that is good for farming.

Devastation comes to Puerto Rico in 2017. Hurricane Maria left homes, vehicles, debris, and fallen trees in its wake.

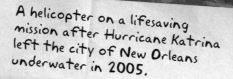

lives at risk from **drowning** or from diseases

Destruction or damage of housing, drains, sewers, dams, roads, and fields

Damaged crops and **undrinkable** freshwater

Drought bakes the soil so hard that it shrinks and cracks. It will no longer absorb water even when rain comes.

In the 1930s, large regions of the United States became so dry that farmland there became a worthless **dust bowl.**

THE HEAT IS ON
A really hot spell of weather is called a heat wave. Most people like to enjoy a sunny day on the beach, but when temperatures soar above 104°F (40°C), it can get dangerous. The body may overheat, causing hyperthermia, or heatstroke.

Dust storms are common in the US prairie and desert states. They can cause breathing complaints, whip up dangerous agricultural chemicals, and can be hazardous to road safety.

DRY AS A BONE
Sometimes it does not rain for months on end, or even years. During a long drought, rivers run dry, and groundwater sinks, so there is little freshwater for drinking, or for watering plants or animals on farms.

DEVILISH DUST
Dust storms are common in deserts or on windy plains where there are few trees. High winds whip sand and dust into the air, darkening the whole sky. It becomes hard to breathe or see, and too easy to lose one's way.

Heatwaves may cause death or illness if the body **overheats,** and long-term **damage** to the skin if it is not protected.

wildfires may break out during droughts, as forests and bushes become very dry.

Lack of water may cause crops and animals to die.

Long periods of drought can mean a risk of famine, illness, and death.

Flash, bang, wallop!

Long ago, people thought that the winds, rain, and sunshine were all the work of gods or goddesses. Thunder and lightning were supposed to be battles fought by angry gods as they crossed the stormy sky. Today we know the science behind the bangs and flashes.

Stay safe

Lightning **strikes** can be deadly. Use these tips to stay safe:

1 If a **storm** is approaching, take cover inside, or in a car with the windows rolled up.

2 If you are caught in the open, find a **low spot** away from trees, fences, and poles.

3 Crouch down, with your hands on your knees, and your **head down** in between your knees.

4 **Do not** make phone calls, unless it is in an emergency, or put up an umbrella.

WHEN LIGHTNING STRIKES

When raindrops inside a cloud freeze and bump into each other, they create electricity. This electricity may build up until the wholecloud fills with electrical charges. A huge spark – lightning – occurs between the two types of electrical charge. It can travel from cloud to cloud, or from cloud to ground.

Positive (+) electrical charges

Negative (–) charges

Positive (+) electrical charges build up on the ground

What is lightning?

When warm, moist air at ground level rises, it may form towering clouds, and a huge electric flash may light up the sky – this is called lightning. It may pass between two clouds, or a long spark can arc between one cloud and the ground.

People have always been awed by the power of thunderstorms. My name, Thor, comes from the Norse word for thunder.

The longest known lightning spark or bolt was recorded in Oklahoma in 2007. It ran over a distance of 200 miles (321 km).

Viewed from space, sheet lightning flashes and flickers over southern Mexico. On the right, the camera has caught a "red sprite," a rarely seen red flash that lights the upper atmosphere.

What is thunder?

Lightning heats the air it passes through to temperatures as high as 54,000°F (30,000°C). This air expands so rapidly it crashes into the air surrounding it faster than the speed of sound. The collision creates a massive shock wave, which goes BOOM!

Track a thunderstorm

Use a timer to work out how far away the lightning is from you.

SUPPLIES

timer on a smartphone, stopwatch, or any watch that can measure seconds • notebook • pen or pencil

WHAT TO DO

1. Start the timer as soon you see the flash.

2. Stop the timer as soon as you hear the thunder.

3. Write down the time in your notebook.

4. Repeat this process as long as the storm continues.

5. Do the math: 3 seconds between the flash and the bang means the lightning is about .6 mile (1 km) away, 6 seconds means it is about 1.2 miles (2 km) away, and so on. Is the storm getting closer or moving away?

WHAT CAN WE LEARN?

Light travels at 186,282.4 miles (299,792.5 km) per second, so you see it pretty much as it happens. But sound travels through the lower atmosphere much slower, at about 1,082.7 feet (330 m) per second.

21

Brrrrr!

Water turns from liquid to solid when it freezes, which happens at 32°F (0°C). In cold weather, puddles, rivers, and lakes freeze over. The weather needs to be really cold before the sea freezes over — find out why this is by completing the experiment on the opposite page.

It's snowing!

Snow forms in clouds, from tiny ice crystals which grow around specks of dust or pollen. The crystals stick to each other in various shapes, falling as snow. In cold weather, the snowflakes reach the ground without melting. Snowflakes on the ground may form a crisp layer, or be blown into great piles called snowdrifts.

In 2010, a NASA satellite recorded the **lowest** known temperature on Earth's surface, in Antarctica: **−138.5°F** (−94.7°C)!

As it falls or settles, snow may be blown into deep drifts by the wind.

Frosty patterns

When the air contains water droplets, tiny ice crystals may form a white coating on freezing cold surfaces, such as blades of grass, twigs, rocks, roofs, or windowpanes. Frost can form beautiful, fern-like patterns.

Frost forms when water vapor freezes on very cold surfaces, turning from gas into solid ice crystals.

Which freezes first – pure water or salty water?

SUPPLIES
freezer compartment • two ice cube trays • two sticky-backed paper labels • tap water • jug • tablespoon • table salt • pen

WHAT TO DO
1. Label one ice cube tray "Tap" and fill it with tap water.

2. In a jug, mix water with about a tablespoon of salt.

3. Label the second tray "Salt" and fill it with the salty water.

4. Place both trays in the freezer compartment of your refrigerator.

5. Which one freezes first?

WHAT CAN WE LEARN?
Use the result of your experiment to answer this question: Why is salt often scattered on roads if freezing weather is forecast?

While hot sunshine scorches the East African savanna, snow covers the top of Mount Kilimanjaro, 19,340.5 feet (5,895 m) above sea level.

Snowy peaks

Mountaintops are nearer to the Sun, yet snow and ice often collect on them. This is because atmospheric pressure drops the higher you go, and this loss of energy results in very cold air on high mountaintops. Even in the hot lands around the equator, mountains may be capped in snow.

Sunshine and heat

Earth is kept warm by radiation from the Sun. This raises the temperature of the air, the land, and the sea. Earth's atmosphere and its clouds act as a blanket, holding in some of that warmth. Ocean currents also affect the weather and the climate.

In the right place

Earth is at just the right distance from the Sun. Any nearer and it would be too hot to support life as we know it. Any further away and it would be too cold.

Planets that can support life are said to be in the habitable zone.

Sun

Too hot

Just right

Too cold

Habitable Zone

The Sun rises over the world's biggest salt flats, at Salar de Uyuni in Bolivia.

Phew!

When we think of heat, we think of a dry, sunny day. But warm air can hold a lot of water vapor, too. Weather that is warm but moist is called humid. Sticky heat is common in tropical regions of the world.

Midnight sun

At the height of the southern summer, the Sun can be seen for 24 hours a day at the South Pole. At that time it is midwinter at the North Pole, and dark for 24 hours a day.

A camera at the Concordia research station in Antarctica tracks the summer Sun over 24 hours.

The **hottest** temperature on record was probably **134°F**, (56.7° C) at Death Valley in California, in 1913.

Sunlight and color

As **sunlight** passes thorugh Earth's atmosphere, it is scattered (deflected).

1. At noon, when the Sun is directly above you, light's path to you is short. There is less time for blue light to scatter, so the sky appears blue.

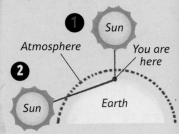

❶ Sun

Atmosphere

You are here

❷

Sun

Earth

2. At sunset, light's path to you is longer. There is more time for blue light to scatter, so the sky appears red.

Measure the temperature

Thermometers are used to measure how hot or cold the air is.

SUPPLIES

plastic water bottle • water • food coloring • clear plastic drinking straw • modeling clay • black marker • large bowl • ice cubes

HOW TO MAKE

1. Fill the bottle right to the top with some warm water and food coloring.

2. Insert the straw about 2 inches (5 cm) into the bottle. Surround it with modeling clay and seal the whole top of the bottle, too.

3. The warm colored water should rise a short way into the straw. Mark the level with the marker.

HOW TO USE

Place the bottle in a bowl of hot water. Watch the liquid expand and rise up the straw. Mark the highest level. Place the bottle in a bowl of ice cubes. Watch the liquid contract and drop down. Mark the lowest level.

❸

❶

❷

Weather science

People have always tried to understand the weather. They have kept a close eye on the sky and tried to work out what a red sky or a misty moon might mean. Today we can rely on weather science, or meteorology. We can measure and record details from around the world.

How do we measure it?

As well as thermometers and rain gauges, a basic **weather station** will also include these instruments:

Barometers forecast weather conditions as air pressure rises or falls, recording it in units called millibars (mb). Electronic pressure sensors are now included in many phones.

Anemometers measure wind speed. You may have spotted them on top of some buildings or bridges – they look like whirling cups or vanes.

Weather electronics

Modern weather science depends on machines that collect data automatically. These might be in weather satellites in space, on ships and buoys in the ocean, fitted to aircraft, or attached to balloons that go into the upper atmosphere. The data is fed back to computers.

And now, the weather...

Satellite data from computers is used to put together the day's weather forecasts on television and the Internet. Forecasts are now more accurate than ever before.

Weather apps on smartphones let you personalize forecasts, wherever you are in the world.

Build a barometer

Barometers don't need to be high-tech. This one uses a balloon and a needle to record changes in air pressure.

SUPPLIES

scissors • balloon • glass jar • rubber band • tape • plastic sewing needle • drinking straw • PVA glue • light card stock • felt-tip pen

HOW TO MAKE

1. Use the scissors to cut off the "neck" of the balloon. Stretch the rest over the top of the jar and secure it tightly with the rubber band.

2. Tape the needle to the end of the straw.

3. Use the glue to stick the needle-free end of the straw on top of the jar.

4. Mark the card with HIGH and LOW as shown, and place it beside the jar. Mark a line at the level of the needle.

Ask an adult for help!

HOW IT WORKS

Air is trapped inside the jar. When the air pressure outside the jar is higher than the pressure inside, it presses down on the balloon and pushes the needle upward. When the pressure outside the jar drops, the air inside the jar pushes the balloon upward, making the needle drop.

HOW TO USE

Mark off the changes to the needle's position every hour or two. Did the air pressure go up or down over the course of a day?

HIGH
—
—
—
LOW

Meteorologists studying the effects of severe thunderstorms prepare to launch a weather balloon.

27

Power up

Humans have made use of weather as a source of natural energy for thousands of years, from storing rainwater for watering crops to using the Sun's warmth to dry crops or preserve food. They made machines to help them, such as windmills, which use wind power to grind grain or pump water.

As wind turbines turn, they generate (make) electricity, which travels along power lines. These may be supported by pylons or buried underground.

Clean and renewable

Today we are using wind, sunlight and water to make electricity. These sources never run out – we say they are renewable. They are also clean. Fuels such as coal, oil, and gas are not renewable and are dirty, too. When we burn them, we create gases that can poison or pollute the air.

Dammed water drives the turbines, generating hydroelectric power.

Wind and water

Turbines are machines that spin around and around to make electricity. They can be made to turn by wind power, and also by the flowing water from tides, waves, or rivers.

Sun power

Electricity made using sunlight is called solar power. Sometimes lenses or mirrors are used to concentrate the Sun's radiation into a powerful beam. This heat can be used to boil water, so that the steam drives turbines. But solar cells can convert sunlight directly into electric power. Panels of these cells can be placed on the roofs of buildings.

At this solar farm in France, large arrays of solar panels capture sunlight. More and more of the world's electricity comes from solar power.

Plants have been using wind power for even longer than humans. A single dandelion plant can produce over 2,000 seeds, to be scattered by the wind!

Make a solar oven

Use the power of the Sun to cook up a tasty snack.

Ask an adult for help!

SUPPLIES

big pizza delivery box • ruler • utility knife • silver foil • sticky tape • heat-safe plastic wrap • black cartridge paper • PVA adhesive • old newspaper • baking tray that fits inside your "oven"

HOW TO MAKE

1. Cut a 3-sided flap, 10 inches (2.5 cm) in from the edge, out of the lid of the pizza box with the knife.

2. Line the underside of the flap with silver foil (shiny side outwards). Wrap the foil around the flap, taping it to the upper side.

3. Place the plastic wrap over the open rectangle of the lid, taping it to the edges.

4. Open the lid and stick black paper to the inside of the box, base and sides.

5. Pack the edges of the box with rolled up newspaper.

6. Place the food you want to heat on a baking tray.

HOW TO USE

When the Sun is at its hottest, place the box on a table outside. Pop the baking tray inside the oven, and prop the foil-covered flap at an angle, so that it reflects the most sunlight possible onto the tray. Your solar oven has a top heat of about 200°F (95°C), and will be great for warming up snacks or precooked food, or melting cheese!

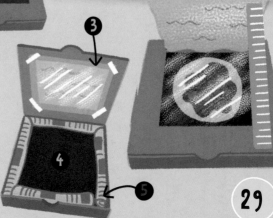

Can climate change?

The weather is always changing, from one day to the next or with the passing seasons. Generally, these changes follow a regular pattern. But over thousands or millions of years a region's climate can change too, or even the climate of the planet as a whole.

What can we do?

These are some simple things you can do at home to help slow climate change:

1. Turn off electrical items when you're not using them.

2. Walk or bike instead of using the car.

3. Reuse and recycle things instead of throwing them away.

4. Reduce food waste.

5. Put on a sweater when you feel a bit cold instead of turning on the heat.

Too hot

In the past, there have been bitterly cold ages, when ice stretched far beyond the polar regions. In between these ice ages, there have been periods when the world became warmer. At the moment, the planet should be slowly moving back towards one of these colder periods, but in fact the planet and its oceans are warming very quickly—too quickly.

The melting of Arctic ice can affect the ability of polar bears to hunt, rest, and breed.

Sun

Solar radiation

Atmosphere

Earth

What about the future?

Global warming could upset weather patterns around the planet, with more violent storms, floods, and drought, melting ice at the poles and raising sea levels. To change course, we need to keep our planet clean and green, using renewable energy. Our survival may depend on it!

Low-lying coral islands such as the Maldives in the Indian Ocean are at risk of disappearing if sea levels rise.

Be a weather historian

Find out if people think that the weather has changed over the years.

SUPPLIES

notebook • pen

WHAT TO DO

1. Interview grandparents or elderly neighbors. Do they think the weather is different from when they were young?

2. Can they remember any big storms, droughts, or floods?

3. Have they noticed any changes to the growing season in gardens or parks? Are there new animals or insects to be seen?

4. Have there been big changes to factories and traffic in their lifetimes?

HOW TO USE

Write down their stories – there may be lessons to be learned. If you interview more than one person, do their memories of big weather events match up?

INDEX

ACKNOWLEDGMENTS

The publishers would like to thank the following artists who have contributed to this book:

Cover Anne Passchier (The Bright Agency)
Insides Anne Passchier and Kim Barnes (The Bright Agency)
All other artwork is from the Miles Kelly Artwork Bank

The publishers would like to thank the following sources for the use of their photographs:
t = top, c = center, b = bottom, l = left, r = right, m = main

Alamy 26–27(m) RGB Ventures/SuperStock
ESA 27(cr) ESA - P. Carril, N. Reul Getty 18(m) Bloomberg, (tr) POOL/Pool; 22(m) Egor Volkov/EyeEm; 24–25(m) Westend61
NASA 5(cr) Scott Kelly, Mark Garcia_Nasa; 6–7(m) NASA Earth Observatory image by Joshua Stevens; 21(t) NASA Earth Observatory

NPL 12–13(m) Christophe Courteau Photo Disc 13(c)
Shutterstock 9(br) Subbotina Anna; 10(b) Juhku, (b) Ondrej Prosicky; 11(cr) jallegri; 12(bl) Sk Hasan Ali; 14(l) Natalya Erofeeva, (c) Nick Pavlakis, (b) Iakov Kalinin; 15(tl) Incredible Arctic, (cr) Tiramisu Studio, (c) Kaido Karner; 16(m) Lysogor Roman, (l) Tonis Valing; 17(m) Minerva Studio, (tl) Glynnis Jones; 19(m) nvelichko, (cr) Caleb Holder; 20–21(m) Vasin Lee; 22(bl) Alexey Kljatov; 23(m) Lyudmila Tetera, (bl) Graeme Shannon; 26(b) Svobodin Anton; 28(m) ssuaphotos, (bl) Alexandru Chiriac; 29(tr) STUDIO M; 30(m) FloridaStock, (b) Nordroden; 31(t) Jag_cz
SPL 24–25(t) NASA/ESA, (br) Alice J. Belling

Every effort has been made to acknowledge the source and copyright holder of each picture. Miles Kelly Publishing apologizes for any unintentional errors or omissions.